Editor

Sara Connolly

Managing Editor

Ina Massler Levin, M.A.

Cover Artist

Brenda DiAntonis

Art Manager

Kevin Barnes

Imaging

James Edward Grace

Rosa C. See

Publisher

Mary D. Smith, M.S. Ed.

Author

Sarah Kartchner Clark, M.A.

Teacher Created Resources, Inc.

6421 Industry Way

Westminster, CA 92683

www.teachercreated.com

ISBN: 978-1-4206-3985-8

©2005 Teacher Created Resources, Inc.

Reprinted, 2009

Made in U.S.A.

Table of Contents

Introduction

Today's children need opportunities to use their brains and to problem solve. The more exposed your students are to problem solving now, the better prepared they will be for the future. Your students need time to think about and explore answers. The book, *Mind Twisters*, is designed to challenge and stretch the brain. These brain teasers will get your students thinking again. This book is a compilation of fun, creative, unique, and challenging experiences for your students. It provides ways to exercise and develop brain power.

The mind twisters can be used to start off the day, or they can be used to enrich the different areas of your curriculum. All of the mind twisters are leveled to be completed by individual learners, although you may choose to pair your students with a partner, if necessary.

Mind Twisters is divided into four sections. These sections are Brain Stretchers, Mathematical Workouts, Problem Solving Puzzlers, and Critical Thinking Connections. Some of the activities are meant for right brain thinking while others are more for left brain thinking. Each section is meant to focus on a different part of the brain to ensure a full brain workout.

Brain Stretchers

The mind twisters in this first section will enrich and increase the vocabulary of your students. These activities will develop such skills as creativity, complexity, analysis, originality, and elaboration. The use of words and language in these activities will also reinforce spelling, reading, and writing skills.

Mathematical Workouts

Activities in this section will improve mathematical skills of your students while reviewing concepts you are already teaching. To complete the mathematical workouts, your students will develop such skills as collection, retention, recall, use of information, and they will further develop mathematical operations.

Problem Solving Puzzlers

The problem solving puzzlers will challenge and push your students. The comfort zone will be redefined as students analyze and solve these puzzles. Though not specific in purpose, your students will continue to develop skills such as risk-taking, trial and error, elaboration, and will require complex thinking skills.

Critical Thinking Connections

It is important to develop different thinking domains, as they have different aims and develop different skills. Critical thinking connections will provide your students with opportunities to examine, clarify, and evaluate an idea, belief or action. Is it reasonable? Students need to infer, hypothesize, generalize, take a point of view, and find solutions. Activities in this section are open-ended and require critical thinking skills to complete. Encourage creativity and thorough investigation as students complete these activities.

Fill in the Blank

Fill in the words that complete each phrase.

1. It's raining cats and _____

2. Hook, line and _____

3. Kindness begins with _____

4. Don't count your chickens before_____

5. Tall, dark, and_____

6. Better safe than _____

7. Save for a rainy _____

8. Healthy, wealthy, and _____

9. Early to bed and early to _____

10. Fool me once, shame on you. Fool me twice, shame _____

11. Only make promises you can_____

12. Don't put all of your eggs in one _____

13. When a door closes, a window _____

14. Rub-a-dub-dub, three_____

15. Good night! Sleep tight! Don't let_____

16. You're going out on a _____

17. Beauty is in the eye of _____

18. A penny saved is a penny _____

19. Beauty comes from _____

20. Honesty is the best _____

4

From One to Ten

Can you turn "one" into "ten" in eleven tries by changing one letter at a time? Only use the clues if you really need to!

O	N	E	
			metal-bearing mineral
			the second word in the contraction "we're"
			painting, sculpture, drawing
			an appendage coming from chest
			to direct toward intended target
			to assist or help
			the cover on a pot
			to light with fire
			to allow or permit
			to gamble
			a boy's name
T	E	N	

Extension

Can you create your own word puzzle? Begin with a word and change it into a different one.
Remember to create clues to give hints.

Decipher the License Plate

Many license plates are personalized with a special message. Can you decode the following license plates?

1. URNIZ

_____

2. IM182DAY

_____

3. IM4IT

_____

4. YRUHRE

_____

5. BLKNBLU

_____

6. BTTRFLI

_____

7. LUVNU

_____

8. PETCHR

_____

9. AU

_____

10. IM4ANTQS

_____

11. CR8Z4U

_____

12. URAQT

_____

13. CRUZN4U

_____

14. EZDUZIT

_____

15. URBZ

_____

16. ICHOT

_____

6

Three of a Kind

Complete each list. All of these are three of a kind. Can you think of any that can be added to the list?

1. Ready, set, _____

2. red, white, and _____

3. tall, dark, and _____

4. reading, writing, and _____

5. Stop, drop, and _____

6. red, yellow, and _____

7. green light, yellow light, _____

8. Larry, Curly, and _____

9. go, fight, _____

10. stop, look, and _____

11. sun, moon, and _____

Can you think of more threesomes? Write three more below.

12. _____

13. _____

14. _____

Classroom Management

Next to each letter of the alphabet, write at least one thing that starts with the letter that you might find in a classroom. *For example: A = Attendance book.* Give yourself a point for each word you can think of for each letter.

A _____   N _____

B _____   O _____

C _____   P _____

D _____   Q _____

E _____   R _____

F _____   S _____

G _____   T _____

H _____   U _____

I _____   V _____

J _____   W _____

K _____   X _____

L _____   Y _____

M _____   Z _____

Same or Similar

Read the words on each line. Explain how they are alike. The first one has been done for you.

1. Australia, Europe, Asia
   These are all continents.

2. Goose, chicken, duck
   _____

3. carrots, potatoes, radishes
   _____

4. tent, sleeping bag, bug spray
   _____

5. hat, muffler, scarf
   _____

6. measles, mumps, polio
   _____

7. jazz, classical, blues, rock n' roll
   _____

8. Jupiter, Neptune, Pluto, Saturn
   _____

9. latte, espresso, tea, coffee
   _____

10. nest, burrow, den
    _____

11. letter, email, phone
    _____

12. soda, water, ice tea, lemonade
    _____

13. knife, pencil, letter opener, nails
    _____

14. cough, sneeze, fever, aches
    _____

What's the Message?

Use the alphabet code to decode the message at the bottom of the page.

A	=	26		N	=	13
B	=	25		O	=	12
C	=	24		P	=	11
D	=	23		Q	=	10
E	=	22		R	=	9
F	=	21		S	=	8
G	=	20		T	=	7
H	=	19		U	=	6
I	=	18		V	=	5
J	=	17		W	=	4
K	=	16		X	=	3
L	=	15		Y	=	2
M	=	14		Z	=	1

Decode this message:

___ ___ ___ ___   ___
14 26 16 22   26

___ ___ ___ ___ ___ ___ ___ ___ ___ ___
23 18 21 21 22   9 22 13 24 22

___ ___ ___ ___ ___!
 7 12 23 26   2

Now decode this message: (Can you do it without using the code?)

___ ___ ___ ___ ___ ___   ___ ___ ___
15 18   8   7 22 13   26 13 23

___ ___ ___ ___ ___.
15 22 26   9 13

Extension: Now create your own message using the code. Write your message on the back of this paper.

Sounds Like an Oxymoron!

An oxymoron is two words that, when put together, mean the opposite of each other. They are contradictory. Match the words in list A with the words in list B to create an oxymoron. Combine the words together on the lines below. A sample has been done for you.

List A		List B	
Bitter	Vaguely	Fire	Favorite
Educational	Open	Court	Best
Sanitary	Conciliation	Aware	Landfill
Fresh	Simply	Secret	Aggressive
Half	Paid	Giant	Choice
Least	Loud	Sweet	Superb
Only	Friendly	Gas	Volunteer
Light	Mild	Television	Park
Liquid	Second	Frozen	Librarian
Little	Industrial	Naked	Curve
Passive	Linear	Rock	Interest

1. _____Bitter Sweet_____
2. _____
3. _____
4. _____
5. _____
6. _____
7. _____
8. _____
9. _____
10. _____
11. _____

12. _____
13. _____
14. _____
15. _____
16. _____
17. _____
18. _____
19. _____
20. _____
21. _____
22. _____

Customer Service

How many words of four or more letters can you make from the word "Accommodations"? You may use each letter only once.

A C C O M M O D A T I O N S

Words with four letters:
Words with five letters:
Words with six letters:
Words with seven letters:
Words with eight or more letters:

What's in the Boxes?

Read the words on the next page. Then match the letters with the correct *synonyms* in the clues. (You will not use all the letters.) Put the five clues together and discover what's in the box.

A	=	pretty
B	=	happy
C	=	cold
D	=	choose
E	=	angry
F	=	like
G	=	beside
H	=	arrange
I	=	automobile
J	=	skinny
K	=	see
L	=	alike
M	=	talk

N	=	pal
O	=	stone
P	=	sad
Q	=	warm
R	=	allow
S	=	jealous
T	=	twig
U	=	educate
V	=	calm
W	=	ship
X	=	nap
Y	=	near
Z	=	portion

What's in the Boxes? *(cont.)*

Clue 1:

_____ _____ _____ _____ _____

depressed furious stick beautiful similar

Clue 2:

_____ _____ _____ _____ _____

stick organize rock permit friend

Clue 3:

_____ _____ _____ _____ _____

envious speak furious similar similar

Clue 4:

_____ _____ _____ _____ _____ _____

enjoy similar rock boat furious permit

Clue 5:

_____ _____ _____

permit furious decide

What is in box #1? _____

Clue 1:

_____ _____ _____ _____ _____ _____

envious beautiful decide decide similar furious

Clue 2:

_____ _____ _____ _____ _____ _____

next to beautiful similar similar rock depressed

Clue 3:

_____ _____ _____ _____ _____

permit furious car friend envious

Clue 4:

_____ _____ _____ _____ _____ _____

organize beautiful similar stick furious permit

Clue 5:

_____ _____ _____ _____ _____ _____

glad permit car decide similar furious

What is in box #2? _____

What's in the Other Boxes?

Read the words on the next page. Then match the letters with the correct *antonyms* in the clues. (You will not use all the letters.) Put the five clues together and discover what's in the box.

A	=	build		N	=	trivial
B	=	dead		O	=	cloudy
C	=	liquid		P	=	happy
D	=	always		Q	=	dishonest
E	=	remembered		R	=	accepted
F	=	foolish		S	=	thoughtful
G	=	harmful		T	=	weak
H	=	bossy		U	=	dependent
I	=	pleasant		V	=	disorderly
J	=	expensive		W	=	interesting
K	=	aged		X	=	deep
L	=	messy		Y	=	intelligent
M	=	wide		Z	=	impatient

What's in the Other Boxes? *(cont.)*

Clue 1:

_____   _____   _____   _____   _____

   sunny   solid   forgot   destroy   serious

Clue 2:

_____   _____   _____   _____

inconsiderate boring uncomfortable narrow

Clue 3:

_____   _____   _____   _____   _____   _____   _____   _____

inconsiderate spotless uncomfortable depressed depressed forgot rejected stupid

Clue 4:

_____   _____   _____   _____   _____

inconsiderate passive uncomfortable serious   stupid

What is in box #3? _____

Clue 1:

_____   _____   _____

 rejected   forgot   seldom

Clue 2:

_____   _____   _____

depressed uncomfortable   forgot

Clue 3:

_____   _____   _____   _____   _____

 safe   rejected   forgot   forgot   serious

Clue 4:

_____   _____   _____   _____   _____

inconsiderate destroy independent solid forgot

Clue 5:

_____   _____   _____   _____

 strong   rejected   forgot   forgot

What is in box #4? _____

All the Vowels

Use the clues to fill in the blanks in the following words. All the words begin and end with a vowel.

1. a ___ ___ ___ e   a red fruit

2. a ___ e   amaze, inspire

3. a ___ ___ ___ e   obtuse, acute

4. e ___ ___ ___ ___ ___ ___ e   to clear out

5. e ___ ___ ___ ___ e   complete, all

6. o ___ ___ e   woodwind instrument

7. o ___ ___ ___ ___ ___ ___ ___ a   brass, woodwinds, strings and percussion

8. o ___ ___ ___ ___ ___ ___ e   to file, put in order

9. i ___ e   frozen water

10. i ___ ___ ___ ___ ___ e   involve, invite

11. a ___ ___ ___ ___ e   niche, bay

12. u ___ ___ ___ ___ ___ ___ a   used to keep dry

13. e ___ ___ ___ ___ ___ ___ ___ e   to do away with

14. e ___ ___ ___ ___ ___ ___ ___ e   to instill confidence

15. a ___ ___ ___ ___ ___ ___ e   rising higher

16. o ___ ___ ___ e   overweight

17. o ___ ___ ___ ___ ___ e   barrier, blockage

18. o ___ ___ ___ ___ e   a fruit and a color

Where Is the Imposter?

In each list below, circle the item that does not belong in the group and explain why on the line provided.

1. Arizona, Alaska, California, New Mexico

   _____

2. Michigan, military, mint, money, Mississippi

   _____

3. April, June, August, November

   _____

4. pine tree, palm tree, Douglas fir tree

   _____

5. bird, train, airplane, spaceship, helicopter, scooter

   _____

6. kilogram, gram, centimeter, hectogram, milligram

   _____

7. corral, croissant, lasso, pueblo, piñata

   _____

8. happy, excited, thrilled, nervous, blissful

   _____

9. Brazil, Chile, Argentina, Mexico

   _____

10. flag, parade, fireworks, snow cones, presents

   _____

Question of the Day

Write a question for each of the following answers.

1. _____

   fruits and vegetables

2. _____

   $23,567.89

3. _____

   an open and shut case

4. _____

   December 7, 1941

5. _____

   the fourteenth amendment

6. _____

   Supreme Court Justice

7. _____

   April 15th of every year

8. _____

   100 calories

9. _____

   lions, tigers, and bears

10. _____

    Maya Angelou

11. _____

    The President of the United States

12. _____

    crackers and cheese

13. _____

    red and orange

Word Association

Circle the words on the right that match with the **bold** words on the left.

1.	**movie**	reel	television	flooring
2.	**France**	Trump Tower	Eiffel Tower	Sears Tower
3.	**president**	validate	verify	veto
4.	**Lake Powell**	Utah	New Mexico	New Jersey
5.	**Yukon**	Hawaii	Texas	Alaska
6.	**mayor**	city	state	nation
7.	**thirteen**	states	countries	colonies
8.	**Clinton**	Nixon	Ford	Gore
9.	**10th President**	John Tyler	James Monroe	John Adams
10.	**El Capitan**	Teton	Yosemite	Yellowstone
11.	**Crater Lake**	longest	widest	deepest
12.	**New York**	apple	pear	orange
13.	**D.C.**	parish	capital	county
14.	**Supreme Court**	district	state	highest
15.	**recycle**	city	agency	bin
16.	**canyon**	forest	river	grand
17.	**ankle**	arm	foot	elbow
18.	**vowel**	fracture	conjugate	consonant
19.	**reward**	renew	reinvigorate	prize
20.	**scuba**	mask	mirror	hammer
21.	**near**	piece	close	speak

What Do You Mean?

An idiom is a phrase or expression that means something different from what the words actually say. What is meant by these idioms? Write an explanation for each group of words.

1. He's in the doghouse now!

   _____

2. Are you getting cold feet?

   _____

3. She really blew her stack!

   _____

4. That baby is like a bull in a china shop!

   _____

5. He is a pain in the neck.

   _____

6. I still feel fit as a fiddle.

   _____

7. Keep a stiff upper lip.

   _____

8. Hold your horses!

   _____

9. He lost his shirt on that deal.

   _____

10. No use crying over spilt milk.

   _____

Compounding the Situation

A compound word is a word that is formed by joining two words. Read the two sentences that will give clues to two words. Join the words together to create the compound word. The first one has been done for you.

1. _campground_ A place you go for a week in the summer (and) the dirt you walk on.

2. _____ Used to cook with on the stove (and) holds the candles on a birthday cake.

3. _____ To see (and) the opposite of in.

4. _____ A man's best friend (and) your home.

5. _____ A fairy pays good money for this (and) used to hold two things together.

6. _____ Found on the beaches (and) made of cardboard.

7. _____ Great or wonderful (and) another word for mom.

8. _____ Opposite of under (and) made from a tree to build a house.

9. _____ A woman (and) a crawling insect.

10. _____ Opposes your finger (and) to pin something up.

11. _____ At the end of your arm (and) wiggle and jiggle.

12. _____ You sleep on it (and) what a clock tells.

13. _____ Pennies are made of this (and) on top of your shoulders.

14. _____ You shake with this (and) plastic or paper.

15. _____ Your fifth "finger" (and) not cursive but . . .

16. _____ In a sandbox (and) comes with thunder and lightning.

17. _____ A sow (and) used to keep sheep inside.

18. _____ April showers bring these (and) used to cook on a stove.

Word Chains

Fill in each blank with a 3-, 4-, 5-, or 6-letter word, depending on the number of blanks given. Each word must begin with the last letter of the preceding word. The word may start with any letter. You may use each word only once. (Race with another student if you are up for a challenge.)

1. _____ _____ _____

2. _____ _____ _____ _____ _____

3. _____ _____ _____ _____ _____ _____

4. _____ _____ _____ _____ _____

5. _____ _____ _____ _____

6. _____ _____ _____

7. _____ _____ _____ _____ _____ _____

8. _____ _____ _____ _____

9. _____ _____ _____ _____

10. _____ _____ _____ _____ _____

11. _____ _____ _____ _____ _____

12. _____ _____ _____

13. _____ _____ _____

14. _____ _____ _____ _____ _____

15. _____ _____ _____ _____

16. _____ _____ _____ _____ _____

17. _____ _____ _____ _____ _____ _____

18. _____ _____ _____

19. _____ _____ _____ _____

20. _____ _____ _____ _____

Clowning Around

Being a clown requires the ability to use a wide range of emotions. Being a good writer requires being able to use a rich vocabulary to express a wide range of emotions. Read the titles in the boxes and make a word bank of at least ten words for each one.

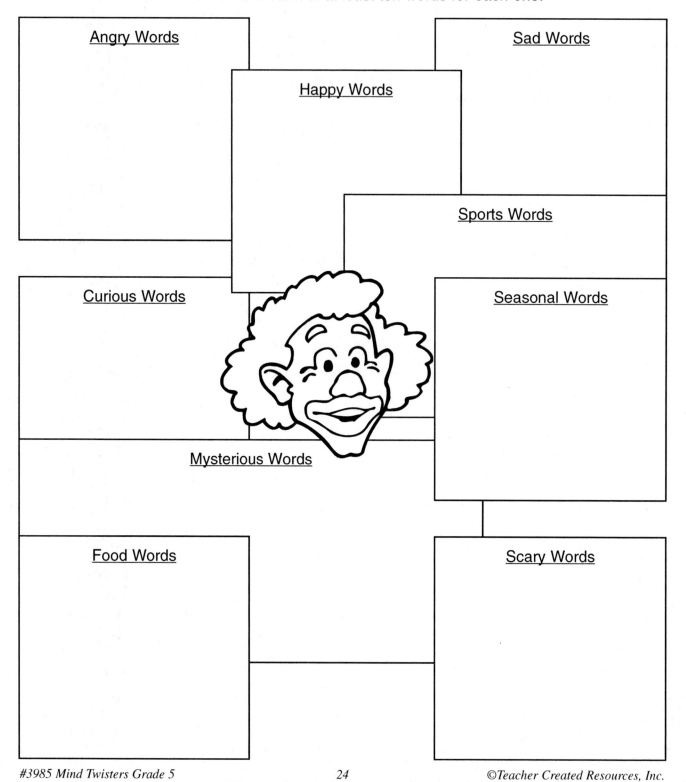

Angry Words

Sad Words

Happy Words

Sports Words

Curious Words

Seasonal Words

Mysterious Words

Food Words

Scary Words

Finding the Solution

Can you find the answers to these word problems? Be sure to explain your answers, if needed.

1. Amy is going to the county fair on Saturday. Each ride costs 50 cents. Amy wants to ride all 19 rides at least once. What is the minimum amount of money she should bring?

2. Farmer John has two more cows than he has horses. If he has eighteen cows, how many horses does he have?

3. If there are three red balls and two blue balls in a bag, what is the probability that you would pull out a red ball. (Remember, you can't peek.)

4. There are 97 fifth graders at Canyon View Elementary School. They are planning a trip to the Andrews Science Observatory. In addition to the students, 4 teachers and 10 parents are going. The observatory charges $1.00 per student and $2.00 per adult. The cost for a bus is $150.00. If each bus holds 45 people, how many buses will be needed?

   What is the total amount of money that will be needed for the trip?

5. Jenny has been asked to make cupcakes for a party at school. The mix that she purchased makes 8 cupcakes. Jenny needs to bring 27 cupcakes. How many mixes does Jenny need to buy? How many mixes would she need if she wanted to make 50 cupcakes?

Finding the Solution *(cont.)*

6. Devin is an avid bird watcher. On Monday he saw 13 birds. On Tuesday, he saw 14 more. On Wednesday, he saw 16, but on Thursday, he didn't see any at all. Then on Friday he saw 14 more birds. How many birds did Devin see during the week, assuming that each bird he saw was a new sighting?

8. You are facing North. Each time you turn, you turn 90 degrees. If you turn 2 times to the right, 1 time to the left, 3 times to the right, 2 times to the right, and 1 time to the left, which way are you facing?

7. Maren is trying to catch 12 crickets to feed her pet bird. It takes her about 3 minutes to catch each one. She has to be at the bus stop in 30 minutes. Does she have enough time to catch all the crickets she needs? Why or why not?

9. What do 10 hundred thousands equal? What about 20 hundred thousands? And 15 hundred thousands?

10. What are the factors of 20?

    What are the factors of 24?

Education Comes First

Which is your favorite subject in school? The six students in this chart all have a favorite. From the clues below, determine the favorite subject of each student. Mark the correct boxes with an "x."

	Math	Writing	Science	Band	Social Studies	Literature
Jacob						
Shiloh						
Caitlyn						
Rebecca						
Jamie						
Shayne						

Clues to Consider:

1. Jacob and Shiloh both like classes involving Language Arts.

2. Jamie could probably tell you what happened in 1945.

3. Shayne needs an instrument but it is not a calculator.

4. Jacob always has his nose in a book.

5. Caitlyn's last experiment lit a fire in the kitchen.

6. Rebecca knows what the square root of two is.

The Sum of Nine

The problem below has over 1900 correct answers. Can you imagine? Solve the problem by arranging the numerals 0, 1, 2, 3, 4, 5, 6, 7, 8, and 9 in the spaces below to make a true equation. You may use each numeral only once. Record at least 14 of the 1900 solutions on the lines provided.

$$\underline{\hspace{1cm}}\ \underline{\hspace{1cm}},\underline{\hspace{1cm}}\ \underline{\hspace{1cm}}\ \underline{\hspace{1cm}}$$
$$+\ \underline{\hspace{1cm}}\ \underline{\hspace{1cm}},\underline{\hspace{1cm}}\ \underline{\hspace{1cm}}\ \underline{\hspace{1cm}}$$

9   9 , 9   9   9

How many different combinations can you find?

1. _____

2. _____

3. _____

4. _____

5. _____

6. _____

7. _____

8. _____

9. _____

10. _____

11. _____

12. _____

13. _____

14. _____

Fill 'er up!

The price of gasoline continues to rise. Solve the problems below to determine the cost of filling up the tank. The first problem has been done for you.

If price per gallon costs . . .

<u>$1.80 per gallon</u>

1. 6 gallons _____

2. 15 gallons _____

3. 12 gallons _____

4. 3 gallons _____

5. 5 gallons _____

6. 9 gallons _____

7. 7 gallons _____

8. 20 gallons _____

9. 2 gallons _____

10. 25 gallons _____

11. 16 gallons _____

12. 26 gallons _____

13. 21 gallons _____

14. 13 gallons _____

<u>$1.76 per gallon</u>

15. 8 gallons _____

16. 15 gallons _____

17. 18 gallons _____

18. 28 gallons _____

19. 22 gallons _____

20. 14 gallons _____

21. 17 gallons _____

22. 21 gallons _____

23. 24 gallons _____

24. 1 gallon _____

25. 11 gallons_____

26. 10 gallons _____

27. 30 gallons _____

28. 38 gallons _____

Extension: Design a math problem using the price of gas per gallon. Solve your problem.

Answer of the Day

In each box below is the answer to a mathematical question. Write a mathematical question for each answer. Be sure to show how you can solve the math problem. Can you find more than one math problem for each answer?

Answer: Only 16 third graders can fit in the bus.

Question:

Answer: There will be four groups of seven dogs

Question:

Answer: Twenty-four dolphins will be able to participate in the show.

Question:

Answer: Each student receives two free passes to the concert.

Question:

Tour De Math

Suppose you are training for a bike race. You will need to train each day for long periods of time. Using the start time provided, can you figure out the miles traveled and the finish time for each training day? Figure the time taken and the miles traveled from start to finish. (Traveling speed is 15 miles per hour.) The first one has been done for you.

Start Time	Miles Traveled		Finish Time	
1. 12:00 A.M.	__45__ miles		3:00 P.M.	__3 hours__
2. 11:00 A.M.	_____ miles		1:00 P.M.	_____
3. 10:00 A.M.	_____ miles		4:00 P.M.	_____
4. 9:00 A.M.	_____ miles		2:00 P.M.	_____
5. 8:00 A.M.	_____ miles		3:00 P.M.	_____
6. 7:00 A.M.	_____ miles		12:00 P.M.	_____
7. 6:00 A.M.	_____ miles		5:00 P.M.	_____
8. 5:00 A.M.	_____ miles		10:00 P.M.	_____
9. 4:00 A.M.	_____ miles		6:00 P.M.	_____
10. 3:00 A.M.	_____ miles		8:00 P.M.	_____
11. 5:30 A.M.	_____ miles		8:30 P.M.	_____
12. 7:30 A.M.	_____ miles		3:30 P.M.	_____

Geometrical Challenge

Are you ready for a geometrical challenge? Each section of the figure below is labeled with a letter. Your task is to find out which whole number goes in each region, and what the color should be. The possible colors are red, orange, yellow, green, blue, and purple. Use the following clues to help you solve this problem.

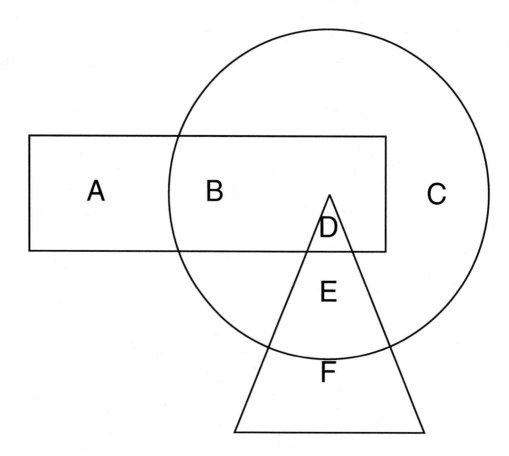

Clues

1. The sum of the triangle is 18.

2. The region that is in all three shapes is colored green.

3. The rectangle has the red, orange, and green regions in it.

4. The yellow region is the number 8.

5. The product of section D and the blue section is 30.

6. The 5 region is green.

7. A is red.

8. The sum of the rectangle is 10.

9. E is blue.

10. The sum of the circle is 21.

11. The sum of A and B is 5.

12. The sum of C and F is 15.

Brain Busters

Test your mathematical abilities by solving the Brain Busters below. All of the answers can be found using basic math skills.

---

1. **Crossing the Street**

   Once there were four boys who wanted to cross a street. They were all on the same side. It was night time and they only had one flashlight between them. Only two boys can cross the street at a time, and anyone who crosses, either one or two people, must always have a flashlight with them. For this to work, the flashlight must be walked back and forth. It cannot be thrown or forgotten. Another issue is that each boy walks at a different speed. A pair must walk together at the speed of the slower boy. Listed below is the amount of time each boy needs to cross the street:

   > Boy #1 needs 1 minute
   >
   > Boy #2 needs 2 minutes
   >
   > Boy #3 needs 5 minutes
   >
   > Boy #4 needs 10 minutes

   (For example, if boy#1 and boy#2 walk across together, they need 2 minutes.)

   The Question: *How can all four boys cross the street in 17 minutes?*

   Write your answer on the back of this page.

---

2. **Hats and Heads**

   Three men were invited to lunch one day. The host places them in a line on three chairs. The men are positioned in such as way that Man #3 can see both Man #1 and Man #2, Man #2 can see only Man #1, and Man #1 can see none of the other men. The host then shows each man 5 hats, 2 of which are black and 3 of which are white. After this, he blindfolds the men, places one hat on each of their heads, and removes the blindfolds again. The host asks if any of the men can determine the color of his hat within one minute. None of the men can see his own hat. After 59 seconds, Man #1 shouts out the color of his hat! He is correct.

   The Question: *What is the color of Man #1's hat, and how does he know?*

Brain Busters II

Keep going! Test your mathematical abilities by solving the Brain Busters below. All of the answers can be found using basic math skills.

---

1. **It Keeps Growing**

   In the middle pond is a patch of moss. The moss doubles in size every day. After exactly 20 days the complete pond will be covered by the moss.

   The Question: *After how many days will half of the pond be covered by the moss?*

---

2. **Shaking Hands**

   Sir John and his wife went to a party where four other married couples were present. Every person shook hands with everyone he or she was not acquainted with. When the handshaking was over, Sir John asked everyone how many hands they shook. Sir John was surprised when he got nine different answers.

   The Question: *How many hands did Sir John's wife shake?*

Mind Numbing Sentences

How many number sentences can you make using combinations of these numbers? You can only use each number once, and you must use all of the numbers. You may use any combination of the number operations (addition, subtraction, multiplication, and division) to create your number sentences. Remember to solve each number sentence.

Examples:

8 ÷ 4 + 13 − 8 x 10 = 70

13 x 8 ÷ 4 + 10 = 36

13	4	8	10

Rearrange the Numbers

Rearrange the numbers below so that 10 sets of three numbers each add up to 20.

16	2	10	5	6
3	1	8	11	6
1	6	4	10	8
17	4	0	8	1
0	5	17	10	15
8	3	4	2	9

Organize the numbers into ten groups below showing the addition problems for each. Each group can only have three numbers. Remember the sum needs to add up to twenty.

The Red Cross

Work out the multiplication problems to find out the name of the founder of the Red Cross.

1. 610
   x6
   ___

2. 523
   x4
   ___

3. 202
   x3
   ___

4. 500
   x7
   ___

5. 943
   x3
   ___

6. 815
   x2
   ___

7. 724
   x4
   ___

8. 718
   x5
   ___

9. 202
   x7
   ___

10. 635
    x3
    ___

11. 955
    x2
    ___

Circle the correct answer:

1.   3150—B
     3006—D
     3660—C

2.   2092—L
     2641—D
     2091—A

3.   636—E
     606—A
     646—I

4.   3501—N
     365—T
     3500—R

5.   2829—A
     2824—B
     2823—C

6.   1638—M
     1630—B
     1646—T

7.   2894—R
     2896—A
     2866—E

8.   3780—W
     3590—R
     3750—X

9.   1614—S
     1444—L
     1414—T

10.   1905—O
     1901—U
     2005—T

11.   1905—P
     1920—M
     1910—N

Answer:

___ ___ ___ ___ ___
1   2   3   4   5

___ ___ ___ ___ ___ ___
6   7   8   9   10   11

Race to the Finish

Mr. Jenson's P.E. class was running a mile long race. Each student in his class had three weeks to prepare. Some of the students had practiced and some had not. Using the clues below, determine each child's place at the end of the race. Mark an "x" in each correct box.

1. Paul, who did not beat Emma, placed higher than Dan and Ellis.
2. Eliza and Ben both placed before Ellis.
3. Dan was not in second place.
4. There was not a tie in the race.
5. Emma received a blue ribbon.
6. Ben was not in fifth place.

	1st	2nd	3rd	4th	5th	6th
Ellis						
Eliza						
Ben						
Dan						
Paul						
Emma						

Extension:

Do you think most of the students in this group prepared for the race? Why or why not? Explain your reasoning

The Next in Line

The number sentences in each exercise follow a pattern. Find the pattern, continue it for two more lines, and then check your answer on a calculator.

76 x 4 = 304	84 x 2 = 168	7 x 8 + 9 = 65
76 x 5 = 380	84 x 22 = 1848	76 x 8 + 8 = 616
76 x 6 = 456	84 x 222 = 18648	765 x 8 + 7 = 6127

_____   _____   _____

_____   _____   _____

Now make up some number sentences of your own that follow a pattern. Be sure to solve each number sentence. You can use a calculator, if needed.

Pattern #1   Pattern #2   Pattern #3

_____   _____   _____

_____   _____   _____

_____   _____   _____

_____   _____   _____

_____   _____   _____

Extension:

Exchange your paper with another student. See if they can discover your patterns.

It's My Birthday!

Sam, Jim, and Jenny all share the same birthday, but they all have different last names. Use this grid and the list of clues to determine who had which flavor of birthday cake and what each person's full name is.

1. The Rollis' daughter loves chocolate.

2. Sam is short for Samantha.

3. No letters from a child's first name appear in a child's last name.

4. The Cook's son had a birthday cake with no food coloring in it.

5. The mother in the Filch family used a vegetable peeler to make the cake.

Family Name	Vanilla Cake	Marble Cake	Carrot Cake

Now create your own problem that can be solved using the grid below. Write clear and concise clues and be sure to double check your clues for accuracy. Solve the puzzle first and then share with another.

Football Fanatic

Have you ever played football before? Use the football field below to help solve the questions below.

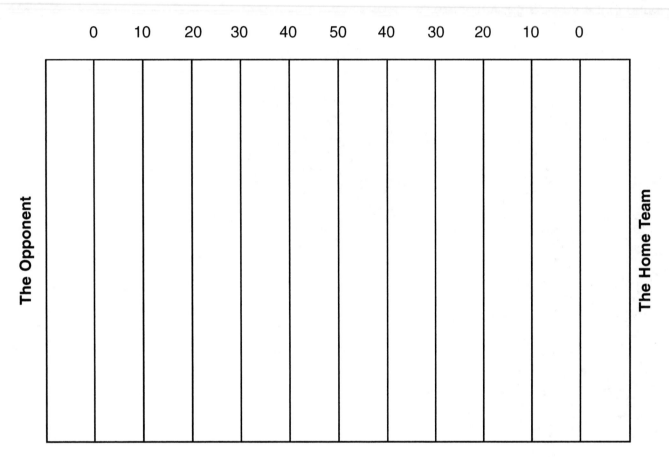

Solve these questions

1. The home team is on the 10-yard line. He runs 15 yards. What yard line is he on now?

2. If the home team is on the 25-yard line and they move the ball five yards each down, where will they be after the third play?

3. The home team catches the ball on their 30-yard line and runs for 50 yards. How many yards does the home team have to run to make a touchdown?

4. The home team fumbles the ball on their 45-yard line. The home team recovers the ball on their 20-yard line. How many yards did the home team lose?

5. When the home team makes a touchdown, they receive 6 points. How many points would have with 4 touchdowns? 8 touchdowns? 6 touchdowns?

What's in the Cube?

This cube below contains 27 cubes. The four sides of each cube alternate light gray and dark gray. The tops and bottoms alternate white and black. Sketch and shade what you think the cube in the very center looks like.

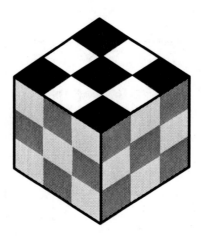

Draw the center cube:

Explain your answer:

Number Chains

To find the answer to this number chain, solve problem # 1. Use this answer in the blank of problem #2. Your answer for number 2 will be the number you put in problem 3. Continue in this manner until you get to problem 7. If your last answer is ninety-nine, then you solved the number chain!

Start

1. 104 + 313	1. 246 + 456	1. 624 + 937
2. _____ + 352	2. _____ + 221	2. _____ + 321
3. _____ − 555	3. _____ + 326	3. _____ − 506
4. _____ + 332	4. _____ − 250	4. _____ − 235
5. _____ − 321	5. _____ − 187	5. _____ − 356
6. _____ + 674	6. _____ + 318	6. _____ + 894
7. _____ − 800 **99**	7. _____ − 1031	7. _____ − 1580

Finish

In the Money

List the dollars and coins you would give each person below to make each amount listed. A sample has been done for you. Draw a picture, if needed, to show the money each person has.

1. $5—Brian has 4 dollars and 15 coins. <u>4 dollars, 5 dimes, ten nickels</u>

2. $4—Lynda has 7 coins and 3 dollars. _____

3. $10—Derek has 9 dollars and 19 coins. _____

4. $6—Melyssa has 5 dollars and 25 coins. _____

5. $4—Laura has 16 coins and 3 dollars. _____

6. $15—Branden has 14 dollars and 6 coins. _____

7. $21—Garett has 10 coins and a 20 dollar bill _____

8. $13—Sean has 1 coin and 12 dollars. _____

9. $15—Cade has 14 dollars and 17 coins. _____

10. $5—Brittany has 4 dollars and 28 coins. _____

Add or Multiply

Place + and/or x signs between the digits so that both sides of each equation are equal.

Hint: You do not need to follow the order of operations for this page.

1.	2	4	2	2	3	=	23
2.	9	9	9	2	2	=	58
3.	5	5	5	4	3	=	162
4.	1	2	3	4	5	=	15
5.	7	6	2	3	8	=	360
6.	5	3	2	4	1	=	41
7.	5	1	1	3	4	=	60
8.	8	1	6	2	8	=	448
9.	2	1	8	9	3	=	93
10.	7	6	5	4	3	=	25

What's the Missing Number?

Use the digits 1 through 9 to complete these number sentences. You may use each digit only once and you must use all digits. The answers already listed do not count as one of the digits from 1 to 9.

A. ☐ x 3 = ☐   ☐
                       – ☐
                       ‾‾‾‾
                        1

    ☐ ÷ 4 = ☐   ☐
                     + ☐
                     ‾‾‾‾

B. ☐ + ☐ = 8   ☐
                       – ☐
                       ‾‾‾‾
                        6

    ☐ ÷ ☐ = 3   9
                       – ☐
                       ‾‾‾‾
                        ☐

C. ☐ + ☐ = 17   ☐
                       – ☐
                       ‾‾‾‾
                        4

    18 ÷ ☐ = ☐   ☐
                     + ☐
                     + ☐
                     ‾‾‾‾
                      13

D. ☐ + ☐ = 13   ☐
                     x ☐
                     ‾‾‾‾
                      9

    ☐ x ☐ = 16   ☐
                     – ☐
                     + ☐
                     ‾‾‾‾
                      6

Word Boxes

Each grid spells three words, names, or acronyms. Each word is written word horizontally and vertically. Fill in the missing spaces in the grid with a letter. Can you find the three words for each grid using the clues given? The first one has been done for you.

1.

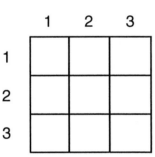

1. seed of a peach
2. feeling sick
3. tender loving care

2.

1. to help or assist
2. anger, rage
3. fox's home

3.

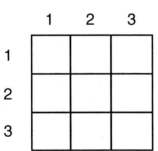

1. to grab or catch
2. carbonated ginger
3. to gamble

4.

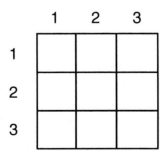

1. baseball hat
2. in the past, a long time _____
3. Edgar Allen _____

Word Boxes *(cont.)*

5.

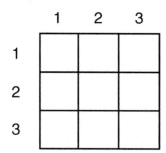

1. case, allotment

2. Spanish word for bear

3. also, in addition

6.

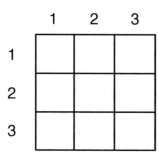

1. to attempt

2. type of bread

3. opposite of no

7.

1. rodent

2. eaten

3. number after nine

8.

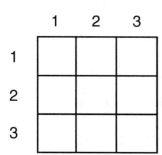

1. type of fish

2. in debt

3. fox's home

Logic Puzzles

Use the grid to help you solve the logic puzzle below. Each letter fits on the grid with a corresponding number. Use the number sentences to help find the number that each letter represents.

1.

A + E = F

G – B = E

C – E = D

B + D = F

Hint: A = 1

E = 4

	1	2	3	4	5	6	7
A	X						
B							
C							
D							
E				X			
F							
G							

2.

A + C = D

G – D = C

E – A = D

B + E = G

F – E = A

Hint: G = 7

C = 3

	1	2	3	4	5	6	7
A							
B							
C			X				
D							
E							
F							
G							X

3. Create your own puzzle. Be sure to give at least one hint.

Number
Sentences:

A	1	2	3	4	5	6	7
B							
C							
D							
E							
F							
G							

Dinner Invitation

Yesterday evening, Joy and her husband invited their neighbors for a dinner at their home. They invited two couples. The six of them sat at a round table. Joy shares the following information with you:

"Ben sat on the left of the woman who sat on the left of the man who sat on the left of Elizabeth. Eve sat on the left of the man who sat on the left of the woman who sat on the left of the man who sat on the left of the woman who sat on the left of my husband.

Jason sat on the left of the woman who sat on the left of Greg. By the way, I did not sit beside my husband."

The Question: What is the name of Joy's husband? Use the circle below for the table and label where everyone sat.

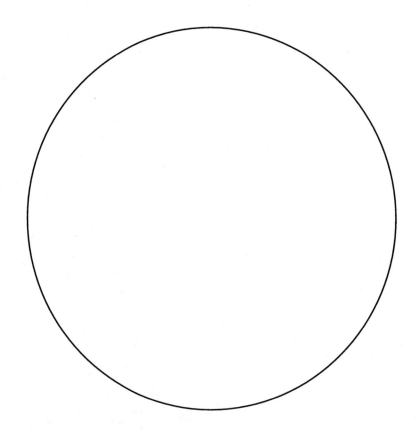

Weather Wise

Hidden in each sentence is a word that a meteorologist might use in a weather report. Each "weather word" can be found either in the middle of a word or by combining the end of one word with the beginning of the next. Underline the "weather word" in each sentence. Here is an example: He i<u>s now</u> in fifth grade. (*weather word = snow*)

1. There was mildew in the bathroom.

2. They had to move the show indoors.

3. The cannon was shot during the Civil War.

4. The tamales were pretty spicy.

5. I'd like to sail the seas on an inner tube!

6. She is unlikely to pass the test.

7. They were about to scold Jess for being late.

8. Heather is learning to speak Spanish.

9. I sprained my ankle at the game.

10. The Thunderbird car is made by Ford.

11. In public, loud noises can be distracting.

12. The monster has torn a door off of its hinges.

13. It has clearly annoyed the dog.

14. Threats of war might encourage the two countries to negotiate.

Running with a Riddle

Can you solve the riddles? Think before you write.

1. Where does August come before July?

2. What is black and white and read all over?

3. What comes next in this pattern o t t f f s s?

4. How many letters are in "the alphabet"?

5. What state is surrounded the most by water?

6. In professional basketball, how many players from a team are on the court at one time?

7. A mother has nine children. She says that half of them are boys. How can this be true?

8. A man was born in 1947. He is healthy and strong today at 27. How is this possible?

9. Sandra is running a race and passes the person in 2nd place. What place is she in now?

10. I can be thrown off a tall building and won't break. I can be thrown into a car, and still I won't break. But, if you throw me in a river or the ocean, I will break into pieces. What am I?

In the Middle

Think of a word or words that contain these letters or fragments of words. The letters belong somewhere in the middle of a word or words. An example has been done for you.

Fragment: ont - c<u>ont</u>ents

1. cess	2. ebo
3. iti	4. aft
5. lish	6. uffi
7. cabu	8. eas
9. ital	10. ette

Unscrambled

Rearrange the letters in each group to create a word. Once each word has been unscrambled, take the first letter of each of the words. Unscramble these letters to determine the final word.

Puzzle #1

Step 1: Unscramble each word.

1. ydfari
2. olgio
3. erefer
4. rotes
5. belritr

Step 2: Now take the first letter of these words and unscramble them to form a new word.

___ ___ ___ ___ ___

Puzzle #2

Step 1: Unscramble each word.

1. debanog
2. labuelmr
3. sedtnirete
4. genaugla
5. netro

Step 2: Now take the first letter of these words and unscramble them to form a new word.

___ ___ ___ ___ ___

Puzzle #3

Step 1: Unscramble each word.

1. raroct
2. parliena
3. renve
4. dsiivino
5. dyytraese

Step 2: Now take the first letter of these words and unscramble them to form a new word.

___ ___ ___ ___ ___

54

Input/Output

Find the rule for each input/output function and fill in the missing spaces.

1. | Input | 3 | 6 | 9 | 12 | 15 |
|---|---|---|---|---|---|
| Output | 36 | 72 | _____ | _____ | _____ |

   The rule: _____

2. | Input | 3 | 5 | 9 | 18 | 20 |
|---|---|---|---|---|---|
| Output | 9 | _____ | _____ | 54 | _____ |

   The rule: _____

3. | Input | 4 | 6 | 8 | 10 | 12 |
|---|---|---|---|---|---|
| Output | 2 | _____ | 4 | _____ | 6 |

   The rule: _____

4. | Input | 6 | 12 | 15 | 21 | 24 |
|---|---|---|---|---|---|
| Output | 19 | 25 | _____ | _____ | _____ |

   The rule: _____

5. | Input | 12 | 14 | 16 | 18 | 20 |
|---|---|---|---|---|---|
| Output | _____ | 36 | _____ | 40 | _____ |

   The rule: _____

6. | Input | 35 | 45 | 55 | 65 | 75 |
|---|---|---|---|---|---|
| Output | 34.5 | _____ | _____ | _____ | 74.5 |

   The rule: _____

The Ultimate Puzzle

Place the numerals 1, 2, 3, 4, 5, 6, 7, 8 and 9 in the puzzle below so that each row whether up, down, or diagonal equals to fifteen. Each number can only be used once.

Hint: The sum of each row equals 15.

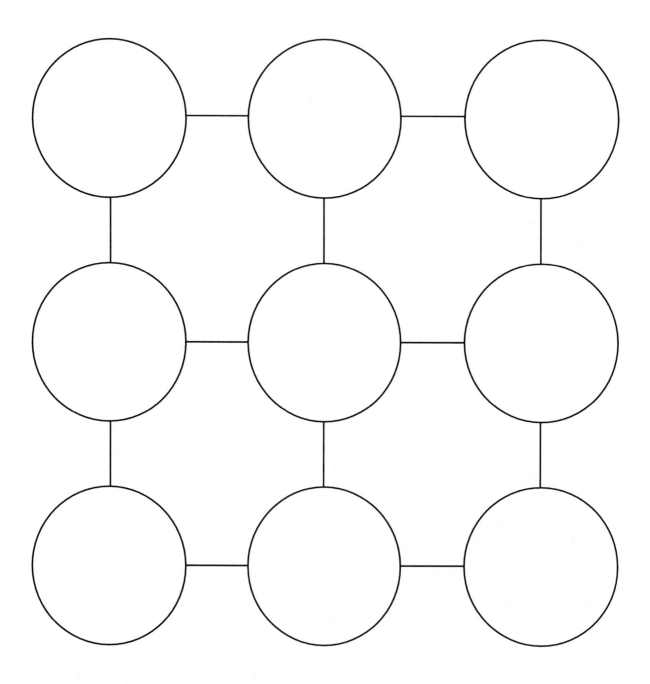

Find the Pattern

Can you find the pattern for each sequence below? Finish the sequence by filling in the spaces.

1.   /   /   *   /   *   /   ___   ___   ___

2.   3   5   7   9   11   13   ___   ___   ___

3.   1   11   21   31   41   51   ___   ___   ___

4.   100   90   80   70   60   50   ___   ___   ___

5.   Q   W   E   R   T   Y   ___   ___   ___

6.   A   B   A   B   B   A   ___   ___   ___

7.   4   8   12   16   20   24   ___   ___   ___

8.   ,   .   ;   '   "   ,   ___   ___   ___

9.   A   S   D   F   G   H   ___   ___   ___

10.   .5   1.5   4.5   13.5   40.5   121.5 ___   ___   ___

Brain Workouts

Are you ready for a test? Follow the directions to solve the puzzles.

1. Read the sentence below:

> Forty Five People Are Going
>
> To The Party Of King Fortwright,
>
> As Long As The King Of Spain
>
> Will Attend With His Queen.

How many times do you see the letter F in the sentence above? Count them only once!
Do not go back and count them again!

2. Michael is standing behind Mitchell, and Mitchell is standing behind Michael. How is this possible?

3. At Jeff's birthday party, his mother brought in the birthday cake. The candles on the cake formed a pattern: red, yellow, red, yellow, blue, red, yellow, blue, purple. The pattern continues adding pink, orange, green, and black candles.

How many candles are on the cake in all? What is the pattern?

4. Joey and Jessica were born on the same day in the same year within a minute apart to the same family, but they are not twins. How can this be?

Two of a Kind

Make a list of words that contain at least two of each letter: two As, two Bs, two Cs, etc.
Examples are ba<u>na</u>na, <u>ba</u>by, a<u>cc</u>ent, and pu<u>dd</u>ing, and <u>e</u>ntir<u>e</u>.

A _____   N _____

  _____

B _____   O _____

  _____

C _____   P _____

  _____

D _____   Q _____

  _____

E _____   R _____

  _____

F _____   S _____

  _____

G _____   T _____

  _____

H _____   U _____

  _____

I _____   V _____

  _____

J _____   W _____

  _____

K _____   X _____

  _____

L _____   Y _____

  _____

M _____   Z _____

  _____

The Letter "X"

The keyboard of a computer was broken when this page was typed. Listed below are familiar phrases, but they are missing some important letters. All of the vowels have been replaced with an "x." Discover what each phrase says and write it correctly on the line.

1. Xxrly tx bxd xnd xxrly tx rxsx.

   _____

2. Dxn't cry xvxr spxlt mxlk.

   _____

3. Yxx cxn't txxch xn xld dxg nxw trxcks.

   _____

4. Twx hxxds xrx bxttxr thxn xnx.

   _____

5. X frxxnd xn nxxd xs x frxxnd xndxxd.

   _____

6. Xll thxt glxttxrs xs nxt gxld.

   _____

7. Nxvxr pxt xff txll txmxrrxw whxt yxx cxn dx txdxy.

   _____

8. Hxstx mxkxs wxstx.

   _____

9. Lxxk bxfxrx yxx lxxp.

   _____

10. Whxn thx cxt's xwxy, thx mxcx wxll plxy.

   _____

Boggle the Mind

Look at the letters in the grids below. How many words can you think of using these letters? Follow the rules below to find the answer.

<u>Rules:</u>

- You must use the central letter of the grid as the beginning of each word.
- No letter can be used more than once in the same word.
- Letters do not need to be connected.
- No proper nouns or slang words allowed.

1.

<u>Words</u>

F	T	O
E	**L**	S
A	M	N

2.

<u>Words</u>

K	L	I
N	**M**	A
T	U	S

3.

<u>Words</u>

E	N	I
U	**T**	R
M	A	Y

Boggle the Mind *(cont.)*

4.

R	A	L
E	**S**	E
N	T	I

Words

5.

F	I	A
O	**W**	G
N	P	S

Words

6.

G	S	A
R	**G**	O
E	P	T

Words

Dot to Dot

This is a classic puzzle that has puzzled people through the years. Can you solve it? Connect the nine dots with four straight lines. You can't lift up the pen between any lines.

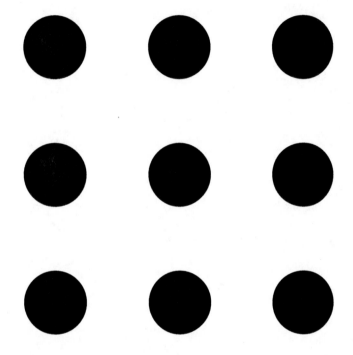

For this puzzle, you need to know how to add! Fill in the magic square so that each row (horizontal, vertical, or diagonal) will add up to 264. You can only use the numbers 1, 6, 8, and 9. There are two possible solutions.

18	99	86	61

Seeing Double

Use the following clues to find words that contain consecutive double letters.

1. An animal from Africa _____

2. gelatin _____

3. A cat in boots _____

4. goes on forever _____

5. Show and . . . _____

6. to the brim _____

7. lost _____

8. jigsaw _____

9. what you do to a leader _____

10. not two or to _____

11. bouncing the basketball _____

12. learning to write _____

13. what your shoe covers _____

14. crackled or scrambled _____

15. nursery rhymes from a mother _____

16. wishing, collects water _____

17. an island state _____

18. type of music _____

19. plausible, it could happen _____

20. served with meatballs _____

Hidden Meanings

Explain the meaning of each box.

FAredCE	BoPussots	insult + <u>injury</u>

1. _____   2. _____   3. _____

r y s	gseg	u p s i d e

4. _____   5. _____   6. _____

LOV	Left out field	i 4 i

7. _____   8. _____   9. _____

trad ition	u PLAT m	bad bad

10. _____   11. _____   12. _____

Hidden Meanings II

Explain the meaning of each box.

I'M you	dribble dribble	knee lights lights
1. _____	2. _____	3. _____
ii dark	long do	1234 me
4. _____	5. _____	6. _____
math the	once 4:50 A.M.	Highway pass
7. _____	8. _____	9. _____
go it it it it	a chance n	search rescue
10. _____	11. _____	12. _____

Catchy Phrases

Explain the meaning of each word or phrase below.

1. the black sheep _____

2. oodles and oodles _____

3. riff raff _____

4. crocodile tears _____

5. puppy dog eyes _____

6. wishy-washy _____

7. bon voyage _____

8. cold shoulder _____

9. limp noodle _____

10. cold feet _____

11. forty winks _____

12. shipshape _____

13. a la carte _____

14. eat crow _____

15. once in a blue moon _____

16. heebie-jeebies _____

17. ballpark figure _____

18. bon appetit _____

19. get out of that sack _____

20. on the dot _____

Milk Moustache

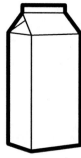

Write at least twenty things you can do with an empty milk carton. Be creative. Go beyond the normal expectations for an empty milk carton.

1. _____

2. _____

3. _____

4. _____

5. _____

6. _____

7. _____

8. _____

9. _____

10. _____

11. _____

12. _____

13. _____

14. _____

15. _____

16. _____

17. _____

18. _____

19. _____

20. _____

A New Idea

What could you do with . . .

A used tire?

_____

_____

_____

_____

_____

Egg cartons that are empty?

_____

_____

_____

_____

_____

Clippings from the lawn?

_____

_____

_____

_____

_____

Name the Countries

Name the countries in which you would find the following cities and geographical features.

1. Amazon River, Rio de Janeiro, rainforest, Salvador

   _____

2. Baja California, Acapulco, Rio Grande, Mazatlan

   _____

3. Great Victoria Desert, Melbourne, Murray River, Sydney

   _____

4. Cape Town, Vaal River, Johannesburg, Drakensberg Mountains

   _____

5. Casablanca, Tangier, Atlas Mountains, Rabat

   _____

6. Madrid, Iberian Mountains, Barcelona, Jucar River

   _____

7. Buenos Aires, Pampas, Parana River, Cordoba

   _____

8. Thames River, London, Liverpool, Edinburgh

   _____

9. Nile River, Cairo, Mount Sinai, Suez Canal

   _____

10. River Shannon, Dublin, Wicklow Mountains, Limerick

    _____

11. Ganges River, New Delhi, Calcutta, Deccan Plateau

    _____

12. Osaka, Mount Fuji, Hiroshima, Suo Sea

    _____

13. Naples, Sicily, Rome, Mount Vesuvius

    _____

Extension: Can you identify the continent to which each of these countries belongs? Use a map or globe, if necessary.

Famous American Firsts

Write the names that correctly answer the following questions. Who was the first . . .

1. American in space? _____

2. American to orbit the earth? _____

3. President of the United States? _____

4. Vice President of the United States? _____

5. Woman to run for President of the United States? _____

6. English child born in America? _____

7. Woman in the United States to receive a medical degree? _____

8. Signer of the Declaration of Independence? _____

9. President of the Red Cross? _____

10. Black soloist to sing with the Metropolitan Opera of New York City?

    _____

11. Pilot to fly an aircraft faster than the speed of sound?

    _____

12. Seamstress to make the first official U.S. flag?

    _____

13. African-American man to play major league baseball?

    _____

14. African-American female Secretary of State?

    _____

15. Native American to play professional baseball, football, and win Olympic gold medals in track and field?

    _____

Forming a Group

Explain what the items in each list below have in common. Be specific. When you have identified the group, then add another member to the group. An example has been done for you.

Marigold, rose, carnation, daisy, tulip (new member)—types of flowers

1. bicycle, train, car, bus, _____

    _____

2. Bears, Vikings, Rams, Cowboys, _____

    _____

3. tiger, lion, panther, jaguar, _____

    _____

4. lime, lemon, orange, _____

    _____

5. September, April, November, _____

    _____

6. dragons, mermaids, unicorns, _____

    _____

7. Lincoln, Grant, Bush, Bush, Ford, _____

    _____

8. Louisiana, Mississippi, Alabama, _____

    _____

9. Maine, Massachusetts, New Jersey, Vermont, _____

    _____

10. plum, peach, pear, _____

    _____

11. chalk, clouds, cotton, _____

    _____

12. Cleveland, JFK, Kennedy, Carter, _____

    _____

72

In Brief

Do you recognize these abbreviations? Write the meaning of each one.

1. bldg. _____

2. lbs. _____

3. St. _____

4. Dept. _____

5. CPR _____

6. FYI _____

7. SASE _____

8. MD _____

9. ASAP _____

10. CEO _____

11. COO _____

12. etc. _____

13. VIP _____

14. IOU _____

15. mph _____

16. N/A _____

17. mfg. _____

18. B.A. _____

19. RR _____

20. B.C. _____

21. esp. _____

Tricky Trivia

How well do you know trivia? All of the trivia questions below have to do with the facts and figures you might know. See how much you know!

1. What building is at 1600 Pennsylvania Avenue?

   _____

2. What is the national motto?

   _____

3. Which President was elected to four terms of office?

   _____

4. Who was the only President who did not win election to either the office of President or Vice President?

   _____

5. Which Great Lake lies entirely in the U.S.?

   _____

6. For whom is America named?

   _____

7. What is Earth's path around the sun called?

   _____

8. In what three forms can matter exist?

   _____

9. What are animals without backbones called?

   _____

10. What was Mark Twain's real name?

    _____

11. What type of book is based on facts?

    _____

12. In the book *Charlotte's Web*, what is the spider's name?

    _____

13. What is the name of the ancient Greek man who wrote a group of fables?

    _____

State the Facts

Name the states that go with each abbreviation.

1. OK _____

2. TN _____

3. VA _____

4. MI _____

5. HI _____

6. MS _____

7. ME _____

8. NJ _____

9. PA _____

10. WA _____

Can you identify the states that correspond with each nickname?

11. What is the Sooner State? _____

12. What is the Pine Tree State? _____

13. What is the Silver State? _____

14. What is the Bluegrass State? _____

15. What is the Hawkeye State? _____

16. What is the Show Me State? _____

17. What is the Copper State? _____

18. What is the Yellowhammer State? _____

19. What is the Natural State? _____

20. What is the Constitution State? _____

Over and Out

	What can you climb into?	What can crawl under?
Write as many things you can think of in the following categories. Draw pictures, if necessary.		
What can you hurdle?	What can you plug in?	What can you fly over?
Who can you call?	What can you name?	What can you itemize?

Which Category?

Divide the following words into groups. Be prepared to explain your decisions in the space provided below.

pepper	rail	package	babies
radio	fourteen	cherries	biscuits
moon	thing	close	pens
croissant	erasers	noodles	joyfully

Categories:

Explanation:

_____

_____

_____

_____

_____

Who's Who in History?

Who are these famous people? For what are they famous? Use the encyclopedia, if necessary.

1. Alexander Graham Bell

   _____

2. Clarence Birdseye

   _____

3. Henry Ford

   _____

4. Benjamin Franklin

   _____

5. George Eastman

   _____

6. Robert E. Lee

   _____

7. Harriet Tubman

   _____

8. Charles Lindbergh

   _____

9. Johnny Appleseed

   _____

10. Susan B. Anthony

    _____

11. Francis Scott Key

    _____

12. George Washington Carver

    _____

13. Sitting Bull

    _____

14. Louisa May Alcott

    _____

Are We Compatible?

What do the two items in each group have in common? Write at least three things for each pair.

diamond and horse	hot dog and book
hill and a well	wheel and handle
biscuit and shoe	chalk and calculator
notebook and tree	crepes and banana bread
snow shovel and vacuum	dog dish and sled

Four Categories

Categorize the words in the box into six categories. Place each word under the correct category. For example, *eating* belongs in the "verb" category. Four words belong under each category

eating	red	Betsy Ross
she	joyfully	furiously
thin	jumped	read
happily	they	softly
it	we	apron
light	ugly	but
envelope	so	yet
lost	and	father

Nouns	Verbs	Pronouns
_____	_____	_____
_____	_____	_____
_____	_____	_____
_____	_____	_____

Conjunctions	Adverbs	Adjectives
_____	_____	_____
_____	_____	_____
_____	_____	_____
_____	_____	_____

Can you write a sentence using one word from each category?

On Location

Think of as many words as you can associate with the words below. Set your clock for five minutes for each category.

A Law Office

An Emergency Room

A Fifth Grade Classroom

The Library

A Museum

Trios

Set your timer for ten minutes (or less) and list as many things as you can think of that come in threes. Can you think of at least twenty?

1. _____   _____   _____

2. _____   _____   _____

3. _____   _____   _____

4. _____   _____   _____

5. _____   _____   _____

6. _____   _____   _____

7. _____   _____   _____

8. _____   _____   _____

9. _____   _____   _____

10. _____   _____   _____

11. _____   _____   _____

12. _____   _____   _____

13. _____   _____   _____

14. _____   _____   _____

15. _____   _____   _____

16. _____   _____   _____

17. _____   _____   _____

18. _____   _____   _____

19. _____   _____   _____

20. _____   _____   _____

Antonym, Homophone, or Synonym

Determine whether or not each set of words is an antonym (a), homophone (h), or a synonym (s). Write the correct answer on the line. Use your brain so you won't be fooled.

1. attempt/endeavor   _____

2. ally/friend   _____

3. joyful/depressing   _____

4. ate/eight   _____

5. vast/minute   _____

6. foe/opposition   _____

7. beautiful/gorgeous   _____

8. praise/preys   _____

9. desire/crave   _____

10. individual/group   _____

11. allowed/aloud   _____

12. stationary/stationery   _____

13. different/unique   _____

14. together/apart   _____

15. rock/stone   _____

16. following/preceding   _____

17. accept/except   _____

18. a loan/alone   _____

Create-a-Sentence

Write as many sentences as you can, using all of the following words: (You can add words to the sentence as needed.)

pot, happily, is, the, sunny, shoe, chef

1. _____

2. _____

3. _____

4. _____

5. _____

6. _____

7. _____

8. _____

9. _____

10. _____

11. _____

12. _____

13. _____

Answer Key

Page 4, Fill in the Blank

1. dogs
2. sinker
3. me
4. they hatch
5. handsome
6. sorry
7. day
8. wise
9. rise
10. on me
11. keep
12. basket
13. opens
14. men in a tub
15. the bed bugs bite
16. limb
17. the beholder
18. earned
19. inside
20. policy

Page 5, From One to Ten

One, ore, are, art, arm, aim, aid, lid, lit, let, bet, ben, ten

Page 6, Decipher the License Plate

1. You are nice
2. I'm 18 today
3. I'm for it
4. Why are you here?
5. Black and blue
6. Butterfly
7. Lovin' You
8. P.E. Teacher
9. Hey you!
10. I'm for Antiques
11. Crazy for you
12. You are a cutie
13. Cruisin' for you
14. Easy does it
15. You are busy
16. Icy Hot

Page 7, Three of a Kind

1. Go
2. Blue
3. Handsome
4. Arithmetic
5. Roll
6. Blue
7. Red Light
8. Moe
9. Win
10. Listen
11. Stars

Page 8, Classroom Management

Answers will vary.

Page 9, Same or Similar

1. continents
2. poultry
3. vegetables that grow underground
4. items you would take camping
5. winter clothes
6. diseases that have vaccines
7. types of music
8. outer planets
9. hot drinks
10. places animals live
11. forms of communication
12. things you drink with ice
13. things that are sharp
14. words associated with being sick

Page 10, What's the Message?

Make a difference today!

Listen and Learn

Page 11, Sounds Like an Oxymoron!

(These may come in a different order.)

1. bitter sweet
2. educational television
3. sanitary landfill

Answer Key (cont.)

4. fresh frozen
5. half naked
6. least favorite
7. only choice
8. light rock
9. liquid gas
10. little giant
11. passive aggressive
12. vaguely aware
13. open secret
14. conciliation court
15. simply superb
16. paid volunteer
17. loud librarian
18. friendly fire
19. mild interest
20. second best
21. industrial park
22. linear curve

Page 12, Customer Service

Answers will vary. Here are some suggestions:
Four-letter words: sand, coma, coda, acts, aids, tons, mats, dams, moat
Five-letter words: comas, comma, Santa, moats, codas, madam
Six-letter words: action, motion, madams
Seven-letter words: actions, motions
Eight-letter words: accommodation, commands,
Nine-letter word: commotion

Page 14, What's in the Boxes?

Box #1—Clue 1: petal, Clue 2: thorn,
Clue 3: smell, Clue 4: flower, Clue 5: red.
Answer: rose

Box #2—Clue 1: saddle, Clue 2: gallop,
Clue 3: reins, Clue 4: halter, Clue 5: bridle.
Answer: horse

Page 16, What's in the Other Boxes?

Box #3— Clue 1: ocean, Clue 2: swim,
Clue 3: slippery, Clue 4: shiny. Answer: dolphin or seal

Box #4—Clue 1: red, Clue 2: pie, Clue 3: green,

Clue 4: sauce, Clue 5: tree. Answer: apple

Page 17, All the Vowels

1. apple
2. awe
3. angle
4. excavate or evacuate
5. entire
6. oboe
7. orchestra
8. organize
9. ice
10. include
11. alcove
12. umbrella
13. eliminate
14. encourage
15. altitude
16. obese
17. obstacle
18. orange

Page 18, Where Is the Imposter?

1. Alaska. It is not a state in the southwest.
2. money. It doesn't begin with the letters MI.
3. August. It doesn't have 30 days.
4. palm tree. It isn't an evergreen tree.
5. bird. It isn't a form of transportation for humans.
6. centimeter. It isn't a measurement of weight.
7. croissant. It isn't a Spanish word.
8. nervous. It isn't a synonym of "joyful."
9. Mexico. It isn't a country in South America.
10. presents. It isn't a word associated with the 4th of July.

Page 19, Question of the Day

Answers will vary.

Page 20, Word Association

1. reel
2. Eiffel Tower

Answer Key *(cont.)*

3. veto
4. Utah
5. Alaska
6. city
7. colonies
8. Gore
9. John Tyler
10. Yosemite
11. deepest
12. apple
13. capital
14. highest
15. bin
16. grand
17. foot
18. consonant
19. prize
20. mask
21. close

Page 21, What Do You Mean?

1. He is in trouble.
2. Are you backing out?
3. She was very angry.
4. The baby is very clumsy.
5. He causes me a lot of problems.
6. I am very healthy.
7. Be brave.
8. Be patient!
9. He lost a lot of money on that deal.
10. Don't cry over past mistakes.

Page 22, Compounding the Situation

1. campground
2. pancake
3. lookout
4. doghouse
5. toothpaste
6. sandbox
7. grandmother
8. overboard
9. ladybug
10. thumbtack
11. handshake
12. bedtime
13. copperhead
14. handbag
15. thumbprint
16. sandstorm
17. pigpen
18. flowerpot

Page 23, Word Chains

Answers will vary.

Page 24, Clowning Around

Answers will vary.

Page 25, Finding the Solution

1. $9.50
2. 16 horses
3. 3 out of 5 or 3/5
4. They will need 3 buses. The cost will be $450 for the buses, $97 for the student entrance fees, and $28 for the adult entrance fees. The total cost will be $575.
5. 4 boxes, 8 x 4 = 32
   7 boxes, 7 x 8 = 56
6. 57 birds
7. No, she doesn't have enough time because it will take her 36 minutes to catch the crickets and she only has 30 minutes before the bus comes.
8. East
9. 1,000,000
   2,000,000
   1,500,000
10. 20—1, 2, 4, 5, 10, 20
    24—1, 2, 3, 4, 6, 8, 12, 24

Page 27, Education Comes First

Jacob—Literature

Shiloh—Writing

Caitlyn—Science

Rebecca—Math

Answer Key *(cont.)*

Jamie—Social Studies

Shayne—Band

Page 28, The Sum of Nine

Answers will vary.

Here are some suggestions:

1. 89,265 + 10,734
2. 28,956 + 71,043
3. 8,437 + 91,562
4. 97,461 + 2,538
5. 67,149 + 32,850
6. 65,210 + 34,789
7. 34,710 + 65,289
8. 4,678 + 95,321
9. 3,412 + 96,587
10. 15,260 + 84,739

Page 29, Fill 'er Up

1. $10.80
2. $27.00
3. $21.60
4. $5.40
5. $9.00
6. $16.20
7. $12.60
8. $36.00
9. $3.60
10. $45.00
11. $28.80
12. $46.80
13. $37.80
14. $23.40
15. $14.08
16. $26.40
17. $31.68
18. $49.28
19. $38.72
20. $24.64
21. $29.92
22. $36.96
23. $42.24

24. $1.76
25. $19.36
26. $17.60
27. $52.80
28. $66.88

Page 30, Answer of the Day

Answers will vary.

Page 31, Tour De Math

2. 30 miles, 2 hours
3. 90 miles, 6 hours
4. 75 miles, 5 hours
5. 105 miles, 7 hours
6. 75 miles, 5 hours
7. 165 miles, 11 hours
8. 255 miles, 17 hours
9. 210 miles, 14 hours
10. 255 miles, 17 hours
11. 255 miles, 15 hours
12. 120 miles, 8 hours

Page 32, Geometrical Challenge

A—3—red

B—2—orange

C—8—yellow

D—5—green

E—6—blue

F—7—purple

Page 33, Brain Busters

1. First, boy #1 and boy #2 walk across the street. This takes 2 minutes.

   Then, boy #1 walks back with the flashlight. This takes 1 minute. Then boy #3 and boy #4 walk across the streeet. This takes 10 minutes. Boy #2 then walks back across the streeet with the flashlight. This takes two minutes. Boy #1 and boy #2 walk across the streeet. This takes 2 minutes. This takes 17 minutes to get all boys across.

   Number sentence: 2 + 1 + 10 + 2 + 2 = 17

2. Man #2 and Man #3 did not give an answer. We can assume from this that both of these

Answer Key *(cont.)*

men do not have enough information. If we start with Man #3, we realize that he must see at least one white hat on the heads of Man #1 or Man #2. This has to be true because if he saw two black hats, he would know that he was wearing a white hat. Man #2 knows that he and/or Man #1 must be wearing a white hat. Since he cannot give an answer, he must be seeing a white hat on Man #1 because if Man #2 could see that Man #1 was wearing a black hat, he would know that he himself wears a white one. Because Man #2 and Man #3 do not say anything, Man #1 knows that he must be wearing a white hat.

Page 34, Brain Busters II

1. Because the moss doubles in size every day, and the pond will be covered in 20 days, and half of the pond will be covered in 19 days. This is just one day before 20 days.

2. It can be assumed that no one at the party shook hands with his or her spouse. Therefore, nobody shook hands with more than eight other people. Sir John got nine different answers and so the answers must be 0, 1, 2, 3, 4, 5, 6, 7, and 8.

   The person who shook 8 hands did not shake hands with his or her spouse and so he/she must be married to the person who shook 0 hands.

   The person who shook 7 hands also shook hands with the person who shook 8 hands (2 handshakes per person). This person must be married to the person who shook 1 hand.

   The person who shook 6 hands, shook hands with all people who also shook hands with the persons who shook 8 and 7 hands (3 handshakes per person). This person also did not shake hands with his/her spouse and so this person must be married to the person who shook 2 hands.

   The person who shook 5 hands must have shaken hands with the persons who shook 6, 7, and 8 hands (a total of at least 4 handshakes per person), but not his or her spouse. This person must be married to the

person who shook 3 hands.

The only person left is the one who shook 4 hands. This must be Sir John's wife.

Page 35, Mind Numbing Sentences

Answers will vary.

Page 36, Rearrange the Numbers

Answers will vary. Here are some suggestions:

16 + 3 + 1

17 + 2 + 1

8 + 8 + 4

4 + 5 + 11

10 + 2 + 8

6 + 6 + 8

9 + 1 + 10

6 + 4 + 10

5 + 0 + 15

3 + 0 + 17

Page 37, The Red Cross

1. 3660
2. 2092
3. 606
4. 3500
5. 2829
6. 1630
7. 2896
8. 3590
9. 1414
10. 1905
11. 1910

Answer: Clara Barton

Page 38, Race to the Finish

Ellis—6th place

Eliza—5th place

Ben—4th place

Dan—3rd place

Paul—2nd place

Emma—1st place

Page 39, The Next in Line

76 x 7 = 532

76 x 8 = 608

84 x 2222 = 186,648

Answer Key *(cont.)*

84 x 22222 = 1,866,648

7654 x 8 + 6 = 61,238

76543 x 8 + 5 = 612,349

Page 40, It's My Birthday

Jim Cook—Vanilla Cake

Jenny Rollis—Marble Cake

Samantha Filch—Carrot Cake

Answers will vary at bottom of the page.

Page 41, Football Fanatic

1. 25 yard line
2. 40 yard line
3. 20 yards
4. 25 yards
5. 24 points, 48 points, 36 points

Page 42, What's in the Cube

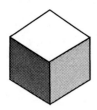

Since each block alternates, we know that the top surface will be white because the top of the cube above it is black. Then, looking at the cubes with white on top, we can see the darker shading is to the left.

Page 43, Number Chains

1. Sum = 417
2. Sum = 769
3. Sum = 214
4. Sum = 546
5. Sum = 225
6. Sum = 899
7. Sum = 99
1. Sum = 702
2. Sum = 923
3. Sum = 1249
4. Sum = 999
5. Sum = 812
6. Sum = 1130
7. Sum = 99
1. Sum = 1561
2. Sum = 1882
3. Sum = 1376
4. Sum = 1141
5. Sum = 785
6. Sum = 1679
7. Sum = 99

Page 44, In the Money

1. 4 dollars, 5 dimes, 10 nickels
2. 3 dollars, 2 quarters, 5 dimes
3. 9 dollars, 9 dimes, 10 pennies
4. 5 dollars, 1 quarter, 3 dimes, 6 nickels, 15 pennies
5. 3 dollars, 2 quarters, 4 dimes, 10 pennies
6. 14 dollars, 3 quarters, 2 dimes, 1 nickel
7. 20 dollars, 10 dimes
8. 12 dollars, 1 silver dollar
9. 14 dollars, 7 dimes, 5 nickels, 5 pennies
10. 4 dollars, 3 quarters, 25 pennies

Page 45, Add or Multiply

1. $2 \times 4 + 2 \times 2 + 3 = 23$
2. $9 + 9 + 9 + 2 \times 2 = 58$
3. $5 + 5 \times 5 + 4 \times 3 = 162$
4. $1 \times 2 \times 3 + 4 + 5 = 15$
5. $7 + 6 + 2 \times 3 \times 8 = 360$
6. $5 + 3 + 2 \times 4 + 1 = 41$
7. $5 \times 1 \times 1 \times 3 \times 4 = 60$
8. $8 + 1 \times 6 + 2 \times 8 = 448$
9. $2 \times 1 + 8 \times 9 + 3 = 93$
10. $7 + 6 + 5 + 4 + 3 = 25$

Page 46, What's the Missing Number?

A. $1 \times 3 = 3$, $7 - 6 = 1$, $8 \div 4 = 2$, $5 + 4 = 9$

B. $7 + 1 = 8$, $8 - 2 = 6$, $9 \div 3 = 3$, $9 - 5 = 4$

C. $8 + 9 = 17$, $5 - 1 = 4$, $18 \div 6 = 3$,

Answer Key *(cont.)*

$2 + 7 + 4 = 13$

D. $6 + 7 = 13$, $9 \times 1 = 9$, $8 \times 2 = 16$,
$5 - 3 + 4 = 6$

Page 47, Word Boxes

2. aid, ire, den

3. nab, ale, bet

4. cap, ago, poe

Page 48, Word Boxes *(cont.)*

5. lot, oso, too

6. try, rye, yes

7. rat, ate, ten

8. cod, owe, den

Page 49, Logic Puzzles

1. A = 1
   B = 3
   C = 6
   D = 2
   E = 4
   F = 5
   G = 7

2. A = 1
   B = 2
   C = 3
   D = 4
   E = 5
   F = 6
   G = 7

Page 50, Dinner Invitation

From the second statement, we know that the six people sat at the table in the following way (clockwise and starting with Joy's husband):

Joy's husband, woman, man, woman, man, Eve

Because Joy did not sit beside her husband, the situation must be as follows:

Joy's husband, woman, man, Joy, man, Eve

The remaining woman must be Elizabeth, and combining this with the first statement, we arrive at the following situation:

Joy's husband, Elizabeth, man, Joy, Ben, Eve

Because of the third statement, Jason and Greg can be placed in only one way, and we now know the complete order: Joy's husband Greg, Elizabeth, Jason, Joy, Ben, Eve. Therefore, the name of Joy's husband must be Greg.

Page 51, Weather Wise

1. mild
2. wind
3. hot
4. icy
5. season
6. sun
7. cold
8. heat
9. rain
10. thunder
11. cloud
12. tornado
13. clear
14. warm

Page 52, Running with a Riddle

1. The dictionary.
2. The newspaper.
3. e, n, t (eight, nine, ten)
4. eleven (You were asked the number of letters in the words "the alphabet.")
5. Hawaii (People often say Florida, California, or Alaska.)
6. Five players on a team.
7. She had all boys. No matter how you look at it, half of them are boys.
8. He was born in Room #1947 in the hospital.
9. Second place. Sandra still needs to pass the person in first place.
10. A tissue.

Page 53, In the Middle

Answers may vary.

1. recess, process
2. ebony, placebo
3. writing, critical
4. raft, draft, after, afternoon

Answer Key *(cont.)*

5. polish, publish, establish
6. sufficient
7. vocabulary
8. peas, please ease, lease, leases
9. capital, marital
10. better

Page 54, Unscrambled

Puzzle #1
1. Friday
2. igloo
3. referee
4. store
5. terrible

Answer: first

Puzzle #2
1. bondage
2. umbrella
3. interested
4. language
5. tenor

Answer: built

Puzzle #3
1. carrot
2. airplane
3. never
4. division
5. yesterday

Answer: candy

Page 55, Input/Output

1. 36, 72, 108, 144, 180—multiply by 12
2. 9, 15, 27, 54, 60—multiply by 3
3. 2, 3, 4, 5, 6—divide by 2
4. 19, 25, 28, 34, 37—add 13
5. 34, 36, 38, 40, 42—add 22
6. 34.5, 44.5, 54.5, 64.5, 74.5—subtract .5

Page 56, The Ultimate Puzzle

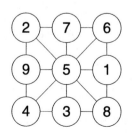

Page 57, Find the Pattern

1. / * /
2. 15, 17, 19
3. 61, 71, 81
4. 40, 30, 20
5. U, I, O—row on keyboard
6. B, A, B
7. 28, 32, 36
8. . ; '
9. J, K, L—row on keyboard
10. 364.5, 1093.5, 3280.5 –multiply by 3

Page 58, Brain Workouts

1. 5 Fs
2. They are standing back to back.
3. This is the pattern:
   red, yellow,
   red, yellow, blue,
   red, yellow, blue, purple,
   red, yellow, blue, purple, pink,
   red, yellow, blue, purple, pink, orange,
   red, yellow, blue, purple, pink, orange, green,
   red, yellow, blue, purple, pink, orange, green, black

   Total Candles: 2 + 3 + 4 + 5 + 6 + 7 + 8 = 35
4. They are in a set of triplets or quadruplets

Page 59, Two of a Kind

Answers will vary.

Page 60, The Letter "X"

1. Early to bed and early to rise
2. Don't cry over spilt milk.
3. You can't teach an old dog new tricks.
4. Two heads are better than one.
5. A friend in need is a friend indeed.
6. All that glitters is not gold.
7. Never put off till tomorrow what you can do today.
8. Haste makes waste.
9. Look before you leap.
10. When the cat's away, the mice will play.

Answer Key *(cont.)*

Page 61, Boggle the Mind

Answers may vary.

1. loft, let, lets, lot, lots, last, lost, loan, lone, loans, lam

2. man, mint, mints, milk, milks, malt, malts, mast, must

3. tire, turn, time, tray, try, train, ten, tan, tin, term

4. seen, sin, sent, salt, seat, silt, slit, seer, sire, see, sea

5. wagon, wagons, wisp, wasp, win, won, wing, wings, wins, want, wig, wigs, wag, wags

6. gag, gasp, gape, gore, got, grapes, grape, gapes, gags, gets, get, gap, gaps

Page 63, Dot to Dot

First Puzzle

Second Puzzle

The are 2 possible solutions:

18	99	86	61
81	66	19	98
69	88	91	16
96	11	68	89

18	99	86	61
66	81	98	19
91	16	69	88
89	68	11	96

Page 64, Seeing Double

1. giraffe
2. Jello
3. puss
4. endless
5. tell
6. full
7. hidden, missing
8. puzzle
9. follow
10. too
11. dribble
12. scribble
13. foot, feet
14. eggs
15. goose
16. well
17. Hawaii
18. classical
19. possible
20. spaghetti

Page 65, Hidden Meanings

1. red in the face
2. Puss in Boots
3. adding insult to injury
4. syrup
5. scrambled eggs
6. upside down
7. endless love
8. out in left field
9. an eye for an eye
10. breaking a tradition
11. platinum
12. too bad

Page 66, Hidden Meanings (cont.)

1. I'm bigger than you
2. double dribble
3. neon lights
4. dark under the eyes
5. long overdue
6. count on me
7. the aftermath
8. once upon a time
9. highway overpass
10. go for it
11. an outside chance
12. search and rescue

Answer Key *(cont.)*

Page 67, Catchy Phrases

1. a bad character in a good group
2. lots and lots
3. people that are considered "trashy"
4. a show of insincere grief
5. sad-looking eyes
6. undecided
7. goodbye, have a good trip
8. treating someone in an unfriendly manner
9. lazy, not up to speed
10. backing out of something
11. a short nap
12. neat and in order
13. separate price for each dish
14. forced to admit something humiliating
15. not very often
16. very nervous, uncomfortable
17. an estimate
18. everybody start eating, have a good meal
19. get out of bed
20. right on time

Page 68, Milk Moustache

Answers will vary.

Page 69, A New Idea

Answers will vary.

Page 70, Name the Countries

1. Brazil
2. Mexico
3. Australia
4. South Africa
5. Morocco
6. Spain
7. Argentina
8. United Kingdom
9. Egypt
10. Ireland
11. India
12. Japan
13. Italy

Page 71, Famous American Firsts

1. Alan Shepard, Jr.
2. John Glenn, Jr.
3. George Washington
4. John Adams
5. Victoria Woodhull
6. Virginia Dare
7. Elizabeth Blackwell
8. John Hancock
9. Clara Barton
10. Marian Anderson
11. Charles Yeager
12. Betsy Ross
13. Jackie Robinson
14. Condoleeza Rice
15. Jim Thorpe

Page 72, Forming a Group

Answers will vary for the additions to each group.

1. means of transportation
2. NFL teams
3. wild cats
4. citrus fruits
5. months with only 30 days
6. make-believe characters
7. Republican presidents
8. Southern U.S. states
9. New England/North East states
10. fruits that begin with "p"
11. items that are white or words that begin with "c"
12. Democratic presidents

Page 73, In Brief

1. building
2. pounds
3. street
4. department
5. Cardio-pulmonary resuscitation
6. for your information
7. self addressed stamped envelope

Answer Key *(cont.)*

8. medical doctor
9. as soon as possible
10. Chief Executive Officer
11. Chief Operating Officer
12. and so forth
13. very important person
14. I owe you
15. miles per hour
16. not applicable
17. manufacturing
18. Bachelor of Arts
19. railroad
20. before Christ
21. especially

Page 74, Tricky Trivia

1. The White House
2. In God we Trust
3. Franklin Delano Roosevelt
4. Gerald Ford
5. Michigan
6. Amerigo Vespucci
7. orbit
8. solid, liquid, gas
9. invertebrates
10. Samuel Clemens
11. nonfiction
12. Charlotte
13. Aesop

Page 75, State the Facts

1. Oklahoma
2. Tennessee
3. Virginia
4. Michigan
5. Hawaii
6. Mississippi
7. Maine
8. New Jersey
9. Pennsylvania
10. Washington
11. Oklahoma
12. Maine
13. Nevada
14. Kentucky
15. Iowa
16. Missouri
17. Arizona
18. Alabama
19. Arkansas
20. Connecticut

Page 76, Over and Out
Answers will vary.

Page 77, Which Category?
Answers will vary.

Page 78, Who's Who in History?

1. He invented the telephone.
2. He was the founder of the quick-freezing process of preserving food.
3. He founded Ford Motor company and was the first to use the assembly line method of production.
4. He invented many items including bifocals, odometer, lightning rod, and the Franklin stove.
5. He invented the Kodak camera.
6. He was leader of the confederate army during the Civil War.
7. She was an influential person who fought to free slaves. She was one of the most successful guides with the Underground Railroad.
8. He was the first solo non-stop flight across the Atlantic Ocean.
9. He was a pioneer who planted apple trees across the United States.
10. She was an advocate of woman's suffrage and is pictured on the one-dollar bill.
11. He wrote the words of "The Star Spangled Banner."
12. He discovered more than 300 uses for peanuts.

Answer Key *(cont.)*

13. He was the Sioux Leader in the battle of the Little Bighorn in which General Custer died.

14. She was the author who wrote *Little Women*.

Page 79, Are We Compatible?

Answers will vary.

Page 80, Four Categories

Nouns—Betsy Ross, apron, envelope, father

Verbs—eating, jumped, read, lost

Pronouns—she, they, we, it

Conjunctions—but, so, yet, and

Adverbs—joyfully, furiously, happily, softly

Adjectives—red, thin, light, ugly

Page 81, On Location

Answers will vary.

Page 82, Trios

Answers will vary.

Page 83, Antonyms, Homophones, or Synonyms

1. s
2. s
3. a
4. h
5. a
6. s
7. s
8. h
9. s
10. a
11. h
12. h
13. s
14. a
15. s
16. a
17. h
18. h

Page 84, Create-a-Sentence

Answers will vary.